Original title:
Tending the Wild Within

Copyright © 2025 Creative Arts Management OÜ
All rights reserved.

Author: Victor Mercer
ISBN HARDBACK: 978-1-80581-841-0
ISBN PAPERBACK: 978-1-80581-368-2
ISBN EBOOK: 978-1-80581-841-0

Nurture the Roots of Desire

In the garden of my whims, I pluck,
With goofy gnomes, I try my luck.
They whisper secrets in the breeze,
While squirrels plot among the trees.

Frog leaps high, he claims the throne,
A merry dance, all on his own.
I dig for dreams in muddy earth,
And smile at chaos, that's my worth.

Rewilding the Inner Self

I donned my hat, my boots with flair,
And skipped through weeds like I don't care.
The raccoons cheer with tiny paws,
As I forget all human flaws.

With butterflies causing a ruckus,
I joined their flight, no need to discuss.
We played hide-and-seek in wild clover,
Who knows? Maybe I'm not done growing over.

The Pulse of Earth's Oldest Song

I hear the earth's tune, oh what a jam,
A chorus led by a funky lamb.
The beats of nature make me sway,
While worms do disco just for play.

With bubbling brooks as my bandmates,
We laugh at time and twist our fates.
We croon, we croak, we all belong,
In this wild wonder, life feels strong.

Awakening the Hidden Earth

Beneath the surface, fun awaits,
With mushrooms chuckling at their fates.
They whisper jokes that make me grin,
As I search for treasures buried in.

The roots below do tango tight,
While ants hold parties through the night.
Awakening spirits of mirth and laughter,
I dance with dirt, my happy ever after.

Whispers from Beneath the Canopy

In the woods where squirrels debate,
I found my shoes gone, oh what fate!
The trees chuckled, their leaves would sway,
As raccoons danced, holding a soirée.

A hedgehog waved with a prickly grin,
Said, "Join our party, come on in!"
But then I tripped, and fell on a vine,
The forest laughed, "Oh, you'll be fine!"

Finding Light in the Shadowed Glen

Down in the glen where shadows creep,
I tried to take a post-lunch nap, deep.
Yet frogs were croaking their funny song,
While chaos reigned, it felt so wrong!

A deer peeked in, with a snickered glee,
"Quiet, please! Can't you see?"
But laughter echoed like bubbles in bloom,
As butterflies danced, dispelling my gloom.

Nature's Secrets in the Quiet Mind

In stillness, thoughts begin to parade,
A raccoon offers his serenade.
"Let's find the snacks," he slyly suggests,
While nature's orchestra plays its best.

The trees whisper gossip, soft and sweet,
About the antics of a wandering beet.
And as I ponder my place in the fray,
A bird chirps loudly, "Oh, come out to play!"

From Concrete to Canopy

From the hard street, to branches that sway,
Where the squirrels throw nuts, sans delay.
They snicker at city folks trying to climb,
As I accidentally slip on a vine—oh, sublime!

The park pigeon coos with a knowing glance,
"Nature's the stage; let's join the dance!"
With laughter infusing each rustling leaf,
I chuckle and grin, and cast aside grief.

Cradle of Forgotten Roots

In a garden of socks, I found a shoe,
A relic of journeys that I never knew.
Worms in the compost engage in a dance,
While the weeds plot a takeover, given a chance.

Old gnomes with their hats stand watch by the vine,
Scheming for sunlight, they sip elderflower wine.
The carrots dream big, they want to be king,
But their tops are too small for such mighty bling.

The Call of the Uncharted Heart

A treasure map drawn in crayon and spice,
Leads to my fridge; oh, isn't that nice?
The pickles are pirates, and cheese is the loot,
I rumble 'neath shelves, wearing nothing but fruit.

A parrot made of lettuce squawks at my snack,
While salsa-tide waves wash over the rack.
I dance with the yogurt, I twirl with delight,
In this quest for adventure, I'm a culinary knight.

Serpents of the Inner Jungle

In the depths of my closet, a snake made of ties,
Stretches and hisses, plotting its rise.
The shirts hold a conference, debating their fate,
While sneakers conspire to open the gate.

Under the bed, dust bunnies spin tales,
Of victories won and of epic fails.
With every new layer of grime, they conspire,
To launch an uprising, that's their secret fire.

Unveiling the Wildflower Heart

An apron of daisies, I wear with pride,
While buttercups whisper and giggle inside.
With spoons as my scepters, I rule over broth,
Dancing with flavors, I don't care for sloth.

A spoonful of laughter, a dash of mischief,
Mixing my potions to mend the rift.
As pans join the party, we twirl and we sway,
In the kitchen of chaos, we'll feast all day!

Embracing the Ferality of Self

In the morning, I skip with glee,
Like a squirrel atop a tree.
Chasing dreams like they're acorns,
Hiding from thoughts that have horns.

With mismatched socks and a loud shirt,
I dance like a wild little dirt.
My inner beast wears fuzzy shoes,
Together we rock all the blues.

The Wilderness Beneath the Skin

Under my skin, a hamster roams,
Building its cozy little homes.
I giggle when it spins its wheel,
A tiny creature, oh what a deal!

My hair is like vines, all a-tangle,
At times I trip on my own ankle.
But isn't life a curious jest?
Closet adventures, I love the best!

Nurturing the Untouched Spirit

In my heart lives a playful fox,
It loves to rummage through old socks.
Nibbles on thoughts like shiny treats,
And takes long walks on fluffy beats.

With a grin that sparkles like dew,
I embrace the quirky me and you.
Wild hair and a cupcake hat,
Living life like a chubby cat.

Secrets of the Inner Grove

In my grove, the trees tell jokes,
About dancing bears and silly folks.
A squirrel's laughter fills the air,
While rabbits weave tales without a care.

Underneath the moon's goofy grin,
I twirl and leap, let the fun begin.
Nature giggles as I spin around,
In this wild world, joy is found!

Rediscovering the Untamed Path

In socks mismatched, I take a stroll,
Among the bushes, I lose control.
A squirrel sidesteps, gives me a wink,
I trip on roots, and spill my drink.

The trees are chuckling, oh what a sight,
As I dodge a branch, it feels so right.
With every tumble, I find my groove,
Nature teaches me how to move.

I dance with flowers, they sway with glee,
While bees buzz loudly and laugh with me.
A misfit in this thriving green mess,
I embrace the chaos, I must confess.

From thorns to laughter, I weave my tale,
With each small fall, I never fail.
The untamed path is one I dare,
For in this wild, I shed my cares.

Threads of Connection in the Wilderness

A vine wraps 'round my leg like a hug,
I yell, "Help!" but it's a playful tug.
Old trees gossip, sharing their lore,
While I'm busy dodging a raccoon chore.

I found a rock that says, "Stay awhile,"
It looks so comfy, with a cheeky smile.
But ants march in, like it's a parade,
As I scurry off, I can't be delayed.

Nature's a canvas, splashed with fun,
Badger and bunny, both come to run.
With laughter swirling like leaves in the air,
I trip over joy, what a wild affair!

To dance with the breeze, I give it a shot,
The laughter of trees, I can't seem to stop.
Each laughter echoes, a shared delight,
In this wild tapestry, I take flight.

A Mosaic of Untamed Whispers

Whispers of grass tickle my nose,
As I wander through wild with mismatched toes.
A rabbit jumps, gives me the side-eye,
While I trip over roots, it's quite a high!

The moon holds court on a silvery night,
And owls hoot loud, 'You got this, alright?'
With twigs as my crown and moss as my seat,
I jest with the shadows, this life is sweet.

When frogs start croaking a quirky song,
I join their band, feeling free and strong.
The fireflies twinkle, they wink and cheer,
In this unscripted play, I have no fear.

Nature's a puzzle, in which we all fit,
And I'm just a piece who loves to commit.
With laughter and wonder, I weave my thread,
In this wild mosaic, I'm joyfully led.

Garden of Untamed Dreams

In a garden sewn with giggles,
We plant our hopes like seeds,
Watering them with chuckles,
Yet they grow into strange beads.

With carrots dressed as clowns,
And spinach in ballet shoes,
We dance around in gowns,
While radishes sing the blues.

The sunflowers wear berets,
As daisies tell tall tales,
While worms plan their cabaret,
And bees send out their emails.

In this patch of silly cheer,
We let our laughter bloom,
For dreams should hold no fear,
And joy will find room!

Whispered Secrets of the Soul

In the attic of our minds,
There's a sock drawer of delight,
Containing all that we can't find,
Like socks that took a flight.

We whisper to the tangled strings,
That play our inner song,
And through the chaos, laughter clings,
As we find where we belong.

With thoughts that jump like frogs,
And giggles that squeak and pop,
We'll turn our worries into logs,
And stack 'em up on top.

In this realm of funny thought,
Our worries take a dive,
For laughter's what we sought,
In the realm where dreams thrive!

Where Heartbeats Roam Free

In the meadows of the heart,
Where beats bounce like a ball,
We chase our dreams as if they start,
With a puppy's joyous call.

Our pulses giggle on the run,
With sunbeams on our toes,
We race and spin just for fun,
In fields where wild joy grows.

Butterflies in top hats sway,
As ladybugs play chess,
While frolicking the day away,
In sweet, unbound finesse.

Here, each heartbeat tells a joke,
With laughter as our guide,
In this land where spirits poke,
We journey side by side!

Echoes of the Untrodden Path

On the road less traveled by,
With shoes that squeak and squeal,
We hum a tune and catch the eye,
Of squirrels that spin a wheel.

The bushes whisper funny ads,
For berries dressed in stripes,
While giggling ants with plaid do pads,
Invite us for some gripes.

Each step's a leap into the fun,
With joy spilling like rain,
While echoes of our laughter run,
Along the silly lane.

In this place of wacky sights,
Where paths weave like a yarn,
We wander free in friendly fights,
With giggles as our charm!

Breaching the Walls of Civilization

In suits and ties we march in line,
But deep inside, our hearts entwine.
With currant scones and endless tea,
We're wild beasts, sipping coffee, whee!

We scroll through life on glowing screens,
Yet crave the thrill of mud and beans.
A power nap beneath great trees,
While squirrels plot our next disease!

The office plant is looking spry,
It dreams of washed-up seaweed pie.
So let's paint our faces, sing a song,
Freedom awaits where we belong!

So here's to those who roam and run,
In rubber boots, we'll have our fun!
With giggles loud and laughter bright,
We'll breach the walls, let's take flight!

Invoking the Spirit of the Wild

The forest calls, a jungle jam,
Singing songs of Uncle Sam.
We dance with mushrooms in our hair,
While raccoons gaze with baffled stare.

A bear swings by, with sense of style,
Wearing shades that make us smile.
With honey drips and berry pies,
We feast 'neath wild and winking skies.

The trees they whisper, 'Join the fun!'
As critters gather, one by one.
A quirky parade, what a wild sight,
Cereal boxes gleam in sunlight!

So grab your taco, like a crown,
Dance with the moon, let's spin around.
We'll invoke a spirit, full of cheer,
In this wild world, there's nothing to fear!

Dances Around the Heart of Nature

Unicorns prance through fields of green,
While squirrels hoard what they've seen.
We twirl with leaves in a gusty spree,
And tumble down, oh woe is me!

Through rivers wide, we laugh and splash,
With rubber ducks we make a dash.
Invisible ink, we paint the sky,
With marshmallow clouds all drifting by.

The daisies giggle, tickled pink,
As we spin circles and start to wink.
What's that behind that leafy fern?
It's just a hobgoblin, wait your turn!

So come on friends, let's dance about,
With wild ideas, there's no doubt.
In nature's heart, we'll lose our cares,
With fumbled grace in messy hares!

Returning to the Original Song

The crickets croon, a night-time beat,
As grasshoppers dance with two left feet.
We strum on sticks, in joyous throng,
Making music where we belong.

The owls hoot backup, wise and clear,
While raccoons clap—it's quite the cheer!
The moonlight shines on all who roam,
Our symphony of joy feels like home!

Backing vocals from frogs and bees,
The trees sway gently with the breeze.
So clap your hands and stomp your feet,
Together we'll create our beat.

With laughter rolling, let's sing along,
In this grand dance, we can't go wrong!
Returning now, with hearts so free,
To the original song, it's pure glee!

The Nature of Internal Flow

In the garden of my mind,
A squirrel steals my lunch.
It hops upon a branch,
Chasing thoughts in a crunch.

A bee buzzes quite loudly,
With ideas to share.
"Pollinate your dreams!"
It cackles in the air.

A butterfly joins in,
Doing pirouettes with glee.
"Life's but a fleeting dance,
So join my jamboree!"

Amidst the green chaos,
The laughter swells and glows.
In this quirky inner place,
My true essence flows.

Rebirthed in the Wild's Embrace

I wore a hat of leaves,
Thought I'd blend with the trees.
Turns out I'm quite the sight,
A fashion faux pas, whee!

A toad croaks out a joke,
While I try to fit in.
"You're stylish in your way!"
Oh, how I love this spin.

With roots wrapped round my feet,
I try to hop and sway.
Just tripping on my thoughts,
Who knew wild could be play?

Nature's whimsy calls me,
In laughter, I am reborn.
A giggle sprouts anew,
In wildness, I am worn.

Reverence for the Unruly Spirit

Oh, unruly spirit, please,
Don't climb that kitchen shelf!
"I'm seeking out adventures,"
It chuckles with great stealth.

Last time you tried to fly,
You ended up in pies.
You hiccupped by the oven,
And filled it with your sighs.

But deep within the chaos,
Your spark ignites the room.
With nature in my heart,
I dance among the blooms.

With each laugh and blunder,
I embrace this silly spree.
For in the wild we wander,
Life's quirks set us free.

The Wilderness of the Inner Child

Oh, what a mess I've made,
With crayons on the wall.
My inner child is grinning,
And ready for a brawl.

I chase behind a rabbit,
"Come play, you fluffy thing!"
But he just twitches ears,
And runs off without a fling.

In a burrow of giggles,
I bounce like grass on air.
Nature tickles my belly,
And shouts, "Let down your hair!"

Amidst the wild and free,
We celebrate the quirks.
For in this untamed space,
Childhood absolutely lurks.

The Pulse of the Ancient Forest

In the depths where the squirrels plot,
Moss grows thick, and secrets are caught.
Trees gossip with a creaky laugh,
As raccoons steal the honeyed staff.

The owls strike a pose, quite refined,
Who knew they'd be so well-defined?
Beneath the ferns, a dance begins,
A waltz of weeds and nature's sins.

Crickets chirp in an offbeat tune,
Belting out their awkward croon.
Even the wind joins in the jest,
Whipping up leaves in a breezy fest.

So here we are, amidst the cheer,
With echoes of nature's quirky sneer.
Embrace the laugh of the lively spree,
And let your spirit move wild and free.

Rekindling the Heart's Wildfire

In the kitchen, pots begin to sway,
The toaster teases with crumbs at play.
Pasta moonwalks on the stovetop high,
As noodles giggle, swirling by.

Flames leap up like squirrels in flight,
But don't fret, they're a friendly sight.
Salt shakers plot to spice up the air,
While spoons and forks have a clanking affair.

The fridge opens wide, with veggies' glee,
Carrots and peas throw a jubilee.
Whether baked or fried, the feast shall bloom,
As chaos reigns in this funky room.

Here we rekindle the silly spark,
With flavors dancing till the dark.
So join our feast, let joy inspire,
And let your heart burst like a campfire.

Chasing Shadows, Finding Light

In the park where shadows loom,
Squirrels dart with a loud 'vroom'.
Chasing tails that twist like knots,
Laughter erupts from all the spots.

As dusk painted faces with funny hues,
A dog in a tutu steals our views.
With each shadow that hops and bounds,
Mirth erupts in jumping sounds.

Under the moon, the fireflies parade,
Dancing like stars, a wild charade.
A whispering wind writes jokes on trees,
While crickets join in with buzzy wheeze.

Chasing shadows, we trip and glide,
With bursts of giggles, nothing to hide.
In the balance of dark and light, let's find,
The joy in the silly we leave behind.

The Oracle of Inner Wilderness

In a cave made of marshmallow fluff,
An oracle grins, quite silly and tough.
With snacks for wisdom, she guides the way,
Fruit snacks and laughter keep worries at bay.

Questions bubble up like soda fizz,
But her answers? Just a playful whizz.
"Today's your day to rock your quirk!
Wear mismatched socks, let humor smirk!"

The ceiling drips with jellybean stars,
Each color a story, from Venus to Mars.
In a fleece blanket cocoon, we engage,
With inner wildness, we take the stage.

So heed this oracle, absurd and bright,
With sprinkles of joy and pure delight.
From silly thoughts to giggle-induced dreams,
Your wild heart's quest is bursting at the seams.

Sheltering the Wild Flowers of Thought

In the garden of my mind, things bloom,
A jumbled mess that smells like perfume.
Thoughts like daisies, dancing in rows,
But wait, is that a weed? Who knows?

Logic's a squirrel, racing around,
Chasing the nuts of wisdom it found.
The petals giggle, their colors delight,
While the thorns hide grumpiness out of sight.

Sunlight tickles, and shadows play,
Ideas stretch like cats in the day.
With laughter, the butterflies flit and swoon,
While I'm busy swatting at a wayward balloon.

So let's cultivate this playful space,
Where thoughts collide in a bright embrace.
A garden of wonders, both wild and sweet,
Where each odd notion finds its own beat.

Beneath the Surface of the Garden

Beneath the soil, a party's in full swing,
Worms dance in circles, oh what a thing!
Gophers gossip about the latest chives,
And disco balls hang from the roots of hives.

Rabbits are rapping, foxes tap their feet,
Moles create tunnels that twist and repeat.
Each underground creature plays their own tune,
While the cactus DJs howl at the moon.

Above, I'm digging, planting with glee,
While critters below plan a wild jubilee.
With mud on my shoes, I wiggle with flair,
Hoping the flowers might join in the air!

So next time you're grumpy, remember this tune,
Life's more fun when you dance with a spoon.
Grab a trowel, join the bizarre, crazy crowd,
And let your garden of laughter grow loud!

The Harmony of Nature's Breath

The trees conspire, whispering sweet,
While mushrooms giggle under my feet.
The wind's a comedian, pulling my hair,
With a punchline soft as an old comfy chair.

Birds gather round for a morning chat,
Chirping about that fancy old hat.
The bees buzz loudly, a boisterous choir,
While I sip coffee, inspired by their fire.

Fragrances mingle, a curious mix,
Of mint and roses, odd little tricks.
The flowers tease each other, what a sight,
As butterflies join in, making it light.

In this woodland concert, there's laughter galore,
With tales of the critters who live to explore.
So tune your heart to this joyful fest,
Nature's humor truly is the best!

Whispering Leaves of Forgotten Truths

Leaves rustle secrets, tales of the past,
Of acorns that dreamt and grew up too fast.
With each crisp sigh, they playfully tease,
"Oh, how we danced, swaying with ease!"

Beneath the branches, humor unfolds,
A squirrel's mischief, a story retold.
He leaps and he tumbles, falls with a thud,
Then scampers back up, proud of his mud.

Old roots yawn wide, awake from their sleep,
As dewdrops giggle, across meadows they leap.
In this realm of green, with laughter and light,
Each leaf whispers wisdom, playful and bright.

So if you feel stuck or lost amid strife,
Remember the joy hidden deep in this life.
For nature's own voice has rhythms and rhymes,
That echo through ages, delights through all times.

Nurturing the Uncharted Soul

In the woods where squirrels chatter,
I dance like nobody's watching,
With a hat made of leaves and twigs,
I'm the king of this wild, no botch-ing!

My shoes are two mismatched socks,
They guide me to streams that run,
Here I sip my wildflower tea,
And try to outrun my own pun!

The Call of Primal Instincts

A raccoon stole my sandwich,
Quite brazen, he took a big bite,
But I chuckled and imagined,
What a thrill to be that light!

I howl at the moon like a pro,
While my neighbor just thinks I'm odd,
Yet in this primal frolic,
I'm truly the nature god!

Embracing Nature's Untamed Embrace

In fields of daisies, I flail,
A love letter to clumsy grace,
I trip over roots, yet prevail,
With a wildflower crown on my face.

Ants march by, giving me side-eyes,
As I wave them a silly salute,
Together we laugh, oh what a prize,
Being silly is just too astute!

Unveiling the Forest Within

With every bark and rustling leaf,
I'll find my inner child, shrieking,
I'd wear a cape made of foliage,
And shout, 'Nature, I am seeking!'

In the shadows, a fox winks sly,
As I trip, flop, and twirl all around,
Who knew losing my balance can fly,
In this forest, pure joy is found!

Reclaiming the Shadowed Glade

In a glade where squirrels dance,
And rabbits prance with their own stance,
The trees gossip, leaves a-flutter,
While mushrooms laugh and start to mutter.

A fox tries yoga, strikes a pose,
With tangled tails and a shy nose,
He falls and rolls, what a big thud,
But up he springs, a mud-bespattered stud!

The owls hoot out a raucous tune,
As raccoons raid the picnic soon,
They tip the basket, spill the grubs,
And leave behind some sticky slubs.

By sunset's blush, they paint the sky,
With all their antics, oh how they fly!
The glade is full of pranks and cheer,
Reclaiming joy is always near!

Dance of the Untamed Soul

In the moonlight's wacky glow,
The critters gather, putting on a show,
A deer in tights, a beetle with flair,
They shimmy and shake while the nights wear bare.

A porcupine spins, all prickles out,
He twirls and swirls, gives a little shout,
His friends all giggle, they join in jest,
A wild ensemble, oh what a fest!

With fireflies glowing, twinkling bright,
The dance goes on, a quirky sight,
Bunnies bobbing to an unseen beat,
An untamed party, oh what a treat!

As dawn approaches, they take a bow,
With laughter echoing, they'll show you how,
In wildest moments, the spirit is whole,
For dance is the rhythm of the untamed soul!

Breath of the Wild Horizon

A breeze whistles through the tall, tall grass,
Where crickets chirp as the moments pass,
Each breath inhaled, a giggle of air,
As clouds drift lazily without a care.

The rabbits leap in a grand parade,
Wearing tiny hats, their plans are made,
With carrots held aloft in pride,
They hop through fields, oh what a ride!

A badger mumbles his morning woes,
With breakfast dreams of berry grows,
He trips on roots, falls in a bush,
Yet somehow laughs with a joyful hush.

So here's to every breath we share,
A wild horizon, with thrills laid bare,
For even in clumsiness, laughter finds,
A way to spark the wild in our minds!

Beneath the Surface of the Heart

Deep in the woods, a secret lies,
Where squirrels trade their acorn spies,
A hidden world of giggles and tricks,
Where everyone's playing various gigs.

A sleepy sloth hangs with utmost grace,
His slow-motion yawn takes up the space,
While owls debate the evening news,
And hedgehogs toast with their tiny brews.

Beneath the heart, a flutter stirs,
As friendship blooms in a flurry of furs,
With wild imagination lighting the way,
It's a rollicking realm where we all can play.

So here we gather, both weird and sweet,
With roots beneath, we joyfully meet,
For in our hearts, the wild does prance,
Encouraging all to join in the dance!

Cultivating the Untamed Essence

In the garden of my mind,
Thoughts sprout like weeds, unconfined.
I accidentally grew a gnome,
Now he's raiding my fridge like it's his home.

Chaos dances with bees,
And my cat joins in with ease.
Together we plot wild schemes,
Like planting pizza trees in our dreams.

A squirrel stole my lunch today,
In a stylish hat, he made his play.
I thought I was the wildest one,
But he's got a crown and thinks it's fun.

With laughter ringing through the night,
We cultivate mischief to our delight.
Untamed spirits twirl and frolic,
Life's a circus, with snacks as the topic.

Harmony of the Hidden Wild

Among the laundry, socks unite,
In a dance that's quite a sight.
They twist and twirl, oh what a mess,
A disco party in my dress.

Beneath the couch, a dust bunny reigns,
King of crumbs, with tiny chains.
He hosts a ball for all his kin,
While I search for the remote within.

The plants conspire to have a shout,
Rooted deep, they won't come out.
"Grow big!" they chant with leafy cheer,
While my pet rock just sits in fear.

In the wildness of my living room,
Each item whispers, "Let's make some zoom!"
Frolicsome chaos wraps me tight,
In this harmony, everything feels right.

Roaring Flames of Hidden Desires

A candle flickers, flames do leap,
Whispering secrets I cannot keep.
"Bake cookies!" it says, "What's the fuss?"
But I burn the dough, now it's a plus.

In my heart, I stoke the fire,
Dreams of pizza, deep-fat fryer.
But the only thing I'd roast is me,
Turned into a crispy, savory spree.

Desires roar like a playful cat,
Chasing yarn, oh where's it at?
I reach for joy in this sweet spree,
But all I find is my lost TV.

With a flip and a flamboyant swoosh,
The flames dance wildly, a smoky whoosh.
Hidden wishes bubble up like so,
In this kitchen grime, I'm quite the show.

The Art of Self-Wilding

In my hair, there's a rogue braid,
A masterpiece that should be laid.
"I'm stylish!" I said with a grin,
But it looks more like a wild squirrel's kin.

Dancing through life with mismatched socks,
I find my rhythm in playful knocks.
Each step is a rebellion, cute and free,
While pigeons coo and cackle with glee.

Mastering the art of having fun,
Even if I'm not the only one.
Today I wore my shirt inside out,
Now I'm a fashion guru, without a doubt.

With giggles echoing, I embrace the day,
In the art of wildness, I lose my way.
But there's beauty in this chaotic twist,
And in the laughter, I find my bliss.

Primal Whispers of the Heart

In the forest of my chuckles,
Bark rumbles, leaves giggle bright.
Squirrels tell me all their secrets,
While I dance under the moonlight.

Mushrooms shout, "Hey, what's the fuss?"
I mumble back, just half awake.
A critter nudges my lunchbox,
Turns out, it's a nibbling snake!

The trees sway in laughter's grip,
As I trip over roots once more.
Nature's jesters make me laugh,
Who knew the wild could be folklore?

My heart's a drum in chaos found,
Beating with joy, so raw and spry.
When I embrace my funny side,
The wilderness grins; oh my, oh my!

Unfurling the Inner Fern

A fern's curl whispers soft delight,
With each unfurling, what a sight!
She winks at me, oh sly green gal,
   Inviting me to join her ball.

Noisy crickets call for a dance,
While I stumble in my trance.
The ground is bumpy, but who cares?
Besides, I've got wild, frizzy hairs!

The sun peeks out to share a cheer,
We shimmy 'round with no sense of fear.
Flora giggles, bugs join in spree,
   Nature's party: wild and free!

Here in the chaos of green we spin,
My heart, a mess, but oh, what a win!
With every twist and turn, we laugh,
Life's a ferny, funny photograph!

Lost in the Grove of Longings

In the grove of whimsical dreams,
A clumsy deer trips on moonbeams.
I search for my wishes, misplaced,
While the bushes burst into raucous haste.

The willow weeps, but I can't tell,
Is it sadness or jest? Oh well.
Berries giggle as I roam near,
Saying, "Pick us, don't shed a tear!"

A dandelion whispers my fate,
"Blow your dreams, or just procrastinate!"
With every puff, a wish takes flight,
Each a journey in the night.

I tumble on laughter, lost yet found,
Nature's humor makes my heart pound.
In this wild, tangled, funny embrace,
I twirl with joy, a comical chase!

Flourish of the Untamed Spirit

A wildflower waves, oh what a sight,
Saying, "Join the fun, it feels so right!"
Thorns tickle as I skip around,
Nature's playground, laughter abound!

Bees buzz tunes of happy glee,
As I jam with a tree, just me.
Roots twist and turn beneath my feet,
Nature's dance is quite the feat!

The sky chuckles, ready to tease,
Clouds drift by, dandy as you please.
I twirl like a fool, arms spread wide,
Embracing the wild, my silly guide.

With every breath, I shed a frown,
The spirit within, no longer down.
So here I stand, a joyful jest,
In this wild heart, I've found my nest!

Reclaiming the Ancestral Voice

In the back of my mind, there's a tale to tell,
Of an old auntie's lizard, who danced quite well.
She'd twirl in the sun, with a wink and a grin,
"Life's just a party, let the wildness begin!"

With a hat made of leaves and boots made of bark,
She'd lead all the critters, from dawn till it's dark.
"Come on, my fine friends, it's a show like no other,
Who knew spinning in circles could spark such a wonder?"

When the moon did arise, with a bosom of light,
She'd dare us to join her, to frolic till night.
"Leave worries behind, and pick up some glee,
Dance with your spirit, it's safe; trust me!"

So here's to that lizard, with rambunctious flair,
Who taught me to laugh without ever a care.
To reclaim every giggle that swells from my core,
I'll channel her wildness and dance, evermore!

The Untold Desires of the Heart

In my chest beats a rhythm, a curious tune,
Like a cat on a keyboard or a jester's balloon.
It whispers and chuckles, with secrets to share,
Of chocolate adventures and wild teddy bears!

I'm longing for pastries adorned with delight,
And sun on my face, a most splendid sight.
My heart holds a carnival, full of sweet jest,
With marshmallows cheering for a s'mores-loving fest!

With giggles like bubbles, they float through the air,
These desires unspoken, so fluffy, so rare.
"I want to be free!" yells my heart with a shout,
"To romp through the fields, where there's giggling about!"

To honor these wishes, I'll follow their lead,
And plant candy gardens, where wild fancies breed.
The heart's funny whispers, I'll let them take flight,
For a parade of pure joy is our heart's true delight!

Mapping the Forgotten Terrain

In the depths of my sock drawer, lies uncharted land,
With mismatched mates plotting, oh, so very grand.
Each hole is a canyon, each wrinkle's a stream,
Adventures await in this playful dream!

A colony of dust bunnies, ready to scheme,
Inventing great tales like a wild circus team.
They ride on the lint roller, so brave and so bold,
"Let's conquer this floor; our story unfolds!"

Mapping my treasure, made of crumbs and cheer,
Where trails of my curiosity lead me to here.
Big dreams fill the corners, like toys left behind,
Retrace keepers of joy, you never can find!

So on this wild journey, with laughter in tow,
I'll navigate socks like a playful pro.
A cartographer's spirit with a smirk and delight,
In this forgotten terrain, adventure ignites!

Songs of the Earth Echoing Within

There's a banter of brambles, a chorus of trees,
A song sung by daisies, carried on the breeze.
They giggle and croon, in the sunlight so bright,
"Join our wild symphony, come dance in the light!"

With each step on the ground, I stomp out a beat,
A flavor of nature that's truly a treat.
The earth sings a jingle, a funky refrain,
Every pebble and puddle joins in on the gain!

The soil does a shuffle, the rocks, they will roll,
As I twirl through the garden, embracing my soul.
"Let's celebrate life!" the wild roses decree,
"Feel the pulse of the planet, just listen and see!"

With echoes of laughter, the earth fills my heart,
In the festival of nature, we're never apart.
So I'll sing with the shrubs, let my wildness unfold,
In a concert of verdure, as jazzy as gold!

The Symphony of Raw Emotions

In the forest, squirrels debate,
Nut strategies that can't wait.
Trees dance to a rhythm quite absurd,
While owls hoot gossip, haven't you heard?

Bears tango with honey jars, pretty bold,
And rabbits argue who's brightest of gold.
The rhythm of nature's a haha spree,
Every branch bending, joyfully free!

A skunk sings the blues with a stinky twist,
While a deer's kick-line can't be missed.
The wind plays the flute as petals sway,
In this musical mess, who needs ballet?

So clap your hands to the chattering trees,
Join the critters, move with ease.
This symphony's a jolly parade,
Where laughter and joy never ever fade.

Revelations from the Edge of the Wilderness

At the edge of the woods, a beaver it seems,
Builds a dam with an eye on dreams.
Mistakes? He shrugs, "I'll just add more sticks!"
His determination? A nature's comedy flick!

Raccoons in masks plan a heist so grand,
For snacks left outside—oh, isn't that planned?
"Do they know we're ninjas of nighttime delight?"
They giggle and prance under the moonlight.

A porcupine slips in a mud-loving dance,
Claims he's just showing off, isn't it chance?
"Look at my quills, so sharp and so wide!"
His friends all laugh but they can't run and hide.

Nature's the judge of each rollicking tale,
With critters who thrive in this quirky detail.
At the edge of the woods, truths can't be missed,
Where humor and chaos always coexist.

Rendezvous with the Primal Shadow

In the twilight glow, shadows tease and play,
Chasing each other, night steals the day.
A coyote howls, it's a late-night show,
While frogs croak puns from the depths below.

An owl spins tales that twist and confound,
Hoots filled with wisdom and jokes all around.
"Who's there?" they ask, as the raccoon grins wide,
"Just me and my snacks, come join this ride!"

Bats flap around with their superhero flair,
Claiming the night with a stylish air.
"Look at us swoop!" they call from above,
It's a rendezvous bursting with chaos and love.

So join in the fun, don't hold back your glee,
The shadows are dancing; just let yourself be!
In this playful ball where the wild hearts dance,
Every chuckle is part of nature's great chance.

The Thrill of Unfurling Dreams

In the early morn, sprouts stretch their heads,
Dreaming of sunshine, coffee, and breads.
A timid worm shouts, "I'll race you all!"
While ladybugs cheer, "Let's have a ball!"

Seeds plan their take-off, "Oh, what a thrill!
To burst from the soil, yes! We have the will!"
A quirky old snail whispers, "Take it slow,
Life's a surreal show if you let it flow!"

Each flower opens with a wink and a sigh,
"Look at me bloom! I just want to fly!"
Butterflies giggle at colors so bright,
Chasing the nectar with pure delight.

So here in this garden of dreams come alive,
We dance with the wind, and feel so alive.
With laughter and cheer, let's rename the game,
The thrill of unfolding—never the same!

Enchantment in the Silenced Grove

In a grove where shadows play,
The squirrels throw nuts in dismay.
A disco party for the trees,
While raccoons swipe snacks with ease.

The mossy dance floor, oh so slick,
The owls hoot out a merry trick.
Sunlight sparkles, laughs abound,
Nature's chuckles all around.

Deep Roots in Shifting Soil

Roots dig deep but wiggle loose,
A worm's a squirmy little moose.
The daisies argue who's the best,
   While dandelions take a rest.

A tumbleweed rolls down the lane,
"Not my fault!" claims a clumsy crane.
The soil giggles, shakes off dust,
While bushes whisper tales of trust.

Reveling in the Untamed Symphony

Crickets sing their off-key song,
While frogs dance like they belong.
The trees all sway, a funky beat,
As nature's jam turns up the heat.

The brook bubbles with laughter's cheer,
"Play it again, bring on the beer!"
A riot of sounds, wild and free,
Nature's band, the best you see!

Awakening the Sacred Wild

A bear in pajamas comes to play,
Spinning tales of his wild day.
The rabbits giggle, rolling 'round,
In a party where joy is found.

A fox dons shades, cool as can be,
Strutting by the old oak tree.
The wild awakens with a cheer,
As laughter rings through every sphere.

Blooming in the Thicket of Self

In a jungle of socks, I lose my way,
The cat steals my lunch, what can I say?
Leaves of my worries, piled up high,
Yet here comes the laughter, oh my oh my!

Hiding behind bushes of laundry so neat,
I stumble upon joy, quite wild and sweet.
The weeds of my doubt, I pull with a grin,
Who knew that wildflowers grew from within?

Squirrels are plotting a food heist tonight,
While I dance with my shadows, feeling just right.
A parade of my quirks, on full display,
In the thicket of self, I'll forever play!

With a butterfly net, I catch all my dreams,
While the fridge hums tunes, like music it seems.
So here in my thicket, I bloom without care,
In the wilderness of me, I find laughter rare!

The Essence of Untouched Horizons

Horizons like pancakes, stacked way up loud,
I flip 'em with joy, I'm both chef and crowd.
With syrupy dreams that are sweet on the tongue,
I dance with the clouds, forever young.

Balloons filled with giggles drift up to the sky,
Pop one, and confetti of laughter flies high!
While unicorns prance in my backyard so bright,
The essence of nonsense brings pure delight.

I chase after rainbows, well, they run kind of fast,
But I trip on my shoelaces, a comic contrast.
The colors collide in a whirl of pure fun,
In this untouched horizon, I'm never outrun.

With a heart full of glitter and socks misaligned,
I scribble my story, uniquely designed.
So lift up your glasses, let's toast to the spree,
In the essence of whimsy, that's where I'll be!

Whispers of the Untamed Heart

My heart sings a tune, oh such nonsense it plays,
With whispers of giggles, it brightens my days.
I wear mismatched socks, like a badge of great pride,
In the wild jungle of life, I bounce like a tide.

While squirrels debate on the best nut to steal,
I munch on my dreams with a hearty meal.
The canary sings songs of the wildest retreats,
And I join in the chorus, swaying my feet.

Chasing after starlight, oh what a wild ride,
I laugh at the shadows that dance by my side.
With a wink to the moon, I embrace the night,
These whispers of joy are my heart's pure delight.

Turning the chaos into a playful spree,
I twirl with abandon, forever carefree.
In the untamed symphony, I play my own part,
For joy is the key to an untamed heart!

Echoes of the Inner Wilderness

In the echoes of laughter, the wildness calls,
It bounces and giggles, it dances and sprawls.
A raccoon in pajamas, what a sight for sure,
In this inner wilderness, adventure's the cure.

I roam through my dreams on a bicycle high,
With feathers and glitter, I reach for the sky.
While wise owls roll their eyes at my schemes,
I find increasing laughter in all of my dreams.

With marshmallow clouds as my fluffy soft guide,
I slide down the rainbows, with joy as my ride.
In the forest of chuckles, I giggle and play,
Echoes of whimsy, brightening my day.

So gather round closely, for wild stories shared,
Of squirrels in sneakers and hearts unprepared.
In this inner haven, I always stand tall,
For echoes of fun, they will never be small!

Threads of the Untamed Fabric

In the garden of my mind, I roam,
Chasing squirrels and gnomes, feeling right at home.
A tangle of thoughts like weeds in the air,
Pulling on thoughts with a giggle and flair.

The sun smiles down as I weave my thread,
Dancing like a scarecrow, my worries all fled.
Grass stains on my knees, mud on my face,
Who knew grown-ups could still dash and race?

I craft a bouquet of quirky ideas,
With petals of laughter, find joy in the tears.
Each stitch a memory, each knot a surprise,
Unraveling tales as the wild spirit flies.

So I prance through the chaos, embracing the fun,
Collecting loose marbles—oh look! There's one!
With wild, woolly hair, I embrace this grand spree,
For the threads of the untamed are wildfully me!

Journey into the Wild Essence

Pack your snacks and paints, away we shall go,
Into forests of giggles where mischief can grow.
With a backpack of stories and snacks to appease,
We'll dance with the daisies and waltz with the bees.

The trees might just chuckle, the brook will join in,
While critters debate about who gets the win.
A frog in a top hat gives us a salute,
"Join our crazy game, be nimble, be cute!"

I trip over roots, as they laugh at my plight,
As I tumble and roll, what a pitiful sight!
Yet each scratch and scrape feels like a badge of fun,
Celebrating the wild, oh, how time flies and runs!

With paint on my hands and joy in my heart,
Every wriggle and giggle, a wild work of art.
So here's to the journey, so zany and free,
Where essence of play is just meant to be me!

The Lushness of Inner Fields

In fields where the marshmallows grow very tall,
I prance like a unicorn—can you hear the call?
With gummy bears grazing and rainbows that dance,
Lose the map; let your heart lead—give joy a chance!

The sun is a cupcake, the clouds are whipped cream,
Who knew inner fields could really be a dream?
With each twist I take, new lands to explore,
A journey of giggles that opens each door.

I tickle the flowers, they giggle in bloom,
And leap over marshmallows, avoiding the gloom.
The lushness around me is ripe with delight,
Where laughter is daylight, and chaos is bright.

So lose all your worries amid the confetti,
Join me in wild fields that are playful and petty.
Together we'll frolic through giggles galore,
In inner landscapes where spirits can soar!

Stirrings of the Forgotten Child

Beneath the adult suit, there's a secret, you see,
A child in a treehouse is longing to be.
With crayons and fingerpaints, it's a crazy mash,
A masterpiece of silly, created in a flash.

With ice cream in hand and a wink of the eye,
I bounce on the bed, as the clouds float on by.
"Let's fly like kites!" I shout to the moon,
And hopscotch with shadows, making mischief our tune.

Whimsical whispers of laughter and glee,
Unravel the threads of my grown-up decree.
For deep in this heart, the echo remains,
Of a child who chose joy, ignoring the chains.

So here's to the stirrings of cheeks full of pie,
And the giggles that sneak in like stars in the sky.
Remember, dear friend, let the child out to play,
For in mischief and laughter, we dance our own way!

Unraveling the Knots of Civilization

In a world all tightly wound,
We trip on shoes, not on ground.
The ties that bind create a fuss,
Yet here we live, just ride the bus.

The maps we draw are full of bends,
Yet all my GPS pretends.
Through tangled thoughts, I search for peace,
Then find forgot where I should cease.

I ask a squirrel for his thoughts,
He's busy hoarding all his nuts.
With laughter shared, we ponder fate,
As squirrels plot to lie in wait.

In knotty lands, our laughter rings,
For who needs rules or fancy things?
We'll brew some tea from wayward leaves,
And toast the chaos that we weave.

Roots That Dance with the Sky

Roots are rumbling, having fun,
They wiggle and giggle in the sun.
'Transplant me, please!' they shout out loud,
Yet stay put in their leafy crowd.

The branches swear they're paragliding,
While roots prepare for some confiding.
"We'll dance with rain!" the flowers say,
And twirl in mud like it's a ballet.

But when the winds decide to howl,
The roots just laugh, "We're here, oh wow!"
"We'll take our breaks and sway with pride,
As trees recall their fanciest glide."

With each breeze, they join the song,
A gospel sung where roots belong.
Though earthy soil is where they play,
Their dreams are sky-high every day.

Mysteries Carried by the Wind

Whispers float in breezy tunes,
They tickle leaves and tease the moons.
"What's the secret?" I inquire,
The wind just grins and lifts me higher.

It swirls with stories, all absurd,
From clumsy birds to gossip heard.
"Catch that leaf!" I hear it shout,
But then it spins, and leaves me doubt.

The wind plays tag with clouds on high,
"Where are you going?" I reply.
It chuckles, puffing in my face,
And sends me chasing at a race.

I ask the breeze for sage advice,
It says just dance, and roll the dice.
For in this game of twist and bend,
The only rule? Just follow 'friend'.

Heartbeats of the Ancient Earth

Underneath the ground, they thrum,
The heartbeat of a rhythm, bum.
Old rocks whisper, "Come and play!"
While mossy gremlins dance all day.

Grassy meadows check the time,
With fluttering clocks that don't quite chime.
Nature's pulse, it skips and hops,
With joyful beat, it never stops.

"Is that a wink?" the trees debate,
As shadows vent and tease their fate.
"Shall we grow taller? Or just recline?"
They laugh aloud, "We're fine, we're fine!"

So if you hear a strange heart glide,
Don't be alarmed, just join the ride.
For life's a dance, a wild affair,
With rhythms that we all can share.

Harvesting Harmony from the Wilderness

In a forest of socks, I found a shoe,
The squirrels laugh, who knew they'd accrue?
A dance with the bees, they buzzed with glee,
While I tripped on a root, oh dear! Not me!

Berries blue and red, I made a pie,
But the raccoons swarmed and gave it a try.
Now they're making plans, and I've lost my bite,
Guess I'm the jester of this woodland night!

Nature's disco ball, the sun starts to shine,
I shake my tail feathers, feelin' divine.
With critters as backup, I perform my song,
In this wacky world, I know I belong!

So let's gather the fruit, make a wild, fun feast,
Invite all the animals, our joy won't cease.
In laughter and chaos, our spirits will swell,
Ah, the wild heart's laughter—I guess it's swell!

Forging Paths through Inner Thickets

Lost in the thickets, where the weeds like to grow,
I found my old fears, all stacked in a row.
A wobbly path formed, where my thoughts like to race,
I laughed at their antics, in this tangled space.

With a map made of giggles, I wandered around,
Found a tree that spoke, with wisdom profound.
"Chop off your worries, they weigh you down,
Join the wild dance, put on that goofy crown!"

Dodging the brambles, I trip with a grin,
A tree gave me sass, said, "Let the fun begin!"
I twirled with the ferns, a wild little laugh,
Got stuck in the branches—a comedic gaffe!

So maybe those thickets, they're not in my way,
They're home to the chuckles, and I'll always stay.
In this funny jungle, the heart's truly free,
Finding joy in the chaos, it's just meant to be!

Breathing Life into Forgotten Dreams

I dusted off a dream, it was covered in moss,
A tiny pink unicorn, oh what a gloss!
With a laugh, it whinnied, stood up on its feet,
"Ready for fun? Let's make this complete!"

We painted the skies with polka dots bright,
Chased away shadows, made day out of night.
Every step felt silly, we danced like a breeze,
Turning every frown into giggling trees!

Those dreams once forgotten, now sprout like a sprig,
They twitch and they wiggle, do the happy jig.
With colorful horses, we glide on a whim,
Unleashing the laughter, the magic won't dim!

So let's breathe in the joy, exhale out the gloom,
Sprinkle bliss everywhere, watch wonder bloom.
In the garden of giggles, life's never a bore,
Let's dance and remember just what dreams are for!

The Garden of Forbidden Thoughts

In a garden of thoughts, where secrets do sprout,
I found a wild pickle, and I had to shout!
"Oh, look at this veggie, I've never met you!
Are you from the land of the veggie crew?"

It giggled back, with a crunch and a smile,
"I'm here to remind you, take a break for a while!
Let's cultivate laughs in this soil of delight,
Where the humor grows heavy, both day and night!"

I watered my worries, they laughed in the rain,
Declared them all jesters, not causing me pain.
We pranced through the daisies, both jolly and free,
The garden was buzzing with sweet harmony!

So let's plant some jokes, and harvest the cheer,
A patch filled with giggles—yes, that's what I steer!
In the garden of wonders, no thought is too odd,
Let's giggle through life, giving smiles a nod!

www.ingramcontent.com/pod-product-compliance
Lightning Source LLC
Chambersburg PA
CBHW070322120526
44590CB00017B/2781